i

QUESTION PRESENTED FOR REVIEW

Does the post removal statute, Title 28 Section 1447, bar the vacatur of a remand order obtained by attorney misconduct and fraud? Plaintiffs were unsuccessful in their attempt to persuade the Sixth Circuit to adopt the reasoning applied by the Fourth Circuit in the case of Barlow v. Colgate Palmolive Co. [F.3d, 2014 WL 6661086], which allowed for vacatur of a remand order under the same circumstances presented in this appeal.

TABLE OF CONTENTS

QUESTIONS PRESENTED i

TABLE OF CONTENTS............................... ii

TABLE OF AUTHORITIES iii

OPINIONS BELOW..1

JURISDICTION.. 1

CONSTITUTIONAL PROVISIONS,
AND STATUTES AT ISSUE 3

STATEMENT OF THE CASE 4

    A. Facts Giving Rise To This Case 4

    B. The State Court Proceedings 5

    C. The District Court Proceedings 7

    D. The Appellate Court Proceedings 12

REASONS WHY CERTIORARI
SHOULD BE GRANTED

1. The District Court Exceeded Its
Statutory Authority 14

2. The Remand Order Created Appealable Collateral Issues............,,,,,..............,,,...,16

3. Review Is Warranted Because Fraud Vitiates Everything............................. 18

4. Review Is Warranted Because Only This Court Can Decide a Circuit Split..... 19

CONCLUSION.. 21

APPENDIX.. 24

    1. Order denying En Banc Review..........23

    2. Order denying Appeal.......................24

    3. Remand Order.................................25

CERTIFICATE OF COMPLIANCE..............23

CERTIFICATE OF SERVICE.....................23

TABLE OF AUTHORITIES

Cases

<u>Barlow v. Colgate Palmolive Co.</u>,

F.3d, 2014 WL 6661086....................16, 17, 19

<u>Kenny v Wal-Mart Stores, Inc., et al.</u>,

2018 WL 650998..15

<u>Thermtron Products, Inc. v. Hermansdorfer</u>,

423 U.S. 336 Id. at 346...........................15, 19

<u>Page v. City of Southfield;</u>

45F.3d 128..16

<u>Cooter & Gell v. Hartmarx Corp.</u>,

496 U.S. 384, 389-90..................................17

<u>Willy v. Coastal Corp.:</u>

503 U.S. 131, 137...................................... 17

<u>Schultz v Butcher,</u>

24 F.3d 626 (1994).....................................17

<u>Kircher v. Putnam Funds Trust</u>

547 U.S 633, at 634…………………………………19

Hazel-Atlas Glass Co. v. Hartford-Empire Co.,

322 U.S. 238……………………………………..…13

Demjanjuk v. Petrovsky,

10 F.3d 338, 348……………………………………..8

Serras v. First Tennessee Bank Nat. Ass'n

875 F.2d 1212, 1214 (6th Cir)……………………..6

Statutes

28 U.S. Code § 1254……………………..………….2

28 U.S. Code § 1446…………..4, 12, 14, 15, 16, 17

28 U.S. Code § 1447……………...………..5, 5, 15

42 U.S. Code § 1983……………………..…………4

15 U.S. Code § 1692i…………………..…………..8

OPINIONS

The order of the United States Court of Appeals for the Sixth Circuit denying rehearing en banc was filed on July 10, 2018.[1] The order of the United States Court of Appeals for the Sixth Circuit denying this appeal was filed on March 28, 2018.[2] The memorandum order of the United States District Court for the Eastern District of Tennessee, granting Respondent's' Motion to Remand, was filed on January 9, 2018.[3] All of which is reprinted in the Appendix hereto, pages 23-35

JURISDICTION

On July 7, 2017, Petitioners removed the State case of Anderson Lumber Co., Inc. v Kinney et al, to the United States District Court for the Eastern District of Tennessee at Knoxville. We alleged, inter alia, that the respondent and others had violated petitioners First Amendment rights, and the due process clause and the equal protection clause of the Fourteenth Amendment to the United

---

[1] Case: 18-5150, DOC 15-1

[2] Case: 18-5150, DOC 10-2

[3] Case 3:17-cv-00288, DOC 12]

States Constitution. On January 9, 2018, the District Court remanded the case to state court.[4] On February 7, 2018, the petitioners timely filed an appeal with the United States Circuit Court of Appeals for the Sixth Circuit, which was dismissed on March 28, 2018. Petitioners timely filed a petition for rehearing en banc with the Sixth Circuit on April 20, 2018, which was dismissed on July 10, 2018. Petitioners have timely filed this Petition and the jurisdiction of this Court to review the Judgment of the Sixth Circuit is invoked under 28 U.S.C. § 1254(1).

CONSTITUTIONAL PROVISIONS AND STATUTES AT ISSUE

First Amendment To The United States Constitution.

Fourth Amendment To The United States Constitution.

Fourteenth Amendment To The United States Constitution.

---

[4] Blount County Circuit Court, Equity Division, Maryville, TN, Case No. E-24747.

28 U.S. Code § 1254(1)

28 U.S. Code § 1446

28 U.S. Code § 1447

42 U.S. Code § 1983

15 U.S. Code § 1692

Constitutional Provisions and Statutes are reprinted in the appendix, pages 23-35.

4

STATEMENT OF THE CASE

I.

A. Facts Giving Rise To This Case

On June 12, 2017, Respondent held an ex parte hearing at state court in which the Petitioners were denied their rights under the First Amendment, and under the due process clause and the equal protection clause of the Fourteenth Amendment to the United States Constitution. At said hearing Petitioners were prevented from presenting their amended answers and counterclaims that were previously filed and pending before the state court. The state court entered an Order dismissing Petitioner Margaret Kinney's original counterclaim which contained a substantive due process property interest in the form of compensatory damages, in the approximate amount of $12,000. On July 7, 2017, pursuant to 28 U.S. Code § 1446(b)(3), Petitioners removed the state case to Federal Court under 42 U.S. Code § 1983, and the Fair Debt Collection Practices Act (FDCPA). On August 7, 2017, in violation of the federal removal statute, respondent held another *ex parte* hearing to set a trial date at state court. On January 9, 2018, the district court remanded the case pursuant to 28 U.S. Code § 1447(c), including the FDCPA claim, without considering the deprivation of our civil and equal rights that occurred at the *ex parte* hearing held on June 12, 2017, which supported removal of the state case.[5]

B. The State Court Proceedings

On November 21, 2012, Respondent sued Petitioners in state court for a debt allegedly incurred on an Anderson Lumber credit account. No evidence of an indebtedness was ever introduced into the record by the respondent for the account sued upon in its complaint. Mr. Landon Coleman, V.P., Anderson Lumber Company, Inc., perjured himself by attesting to an alleged debt owed by the Petitioners in his Sworn Account. Petitioners have properly introduced into the record sworn affidavits disputing every allegation of fact relevant to the alleged debt specified in respondent's state complaint. The respondent has failed to establish its prima facie showing needed to procure personal jurisdiction over the Petitioners in state court that comports with the Fourteenth

---

[5] A trial date has been set by the respondent in state court for October 16, 2018

Amendment.[6] Subsequently, the state court's exercise of personal jurisdiction over the Kinneys violates the requirements of due process.

At a hearing held in District Court, the respondent asserted to the Honorable Bruce H. Guyton, Chief Magistrate Judge of the District Court for the Eastern Division of Tennessee, that it had the documentation needed to support its state claim, but then failed to produce the documentation when ordered to do so by the district court. The Respondent deliberately and wrongfully concealed the factual predicate to Petitioners' claims in order to unlawfully procure and maintain jurisdiction over the Kinneys in state court. The state court has shown prejudice to the petitioners, and favor to the respondent and their counsel, that has risen to a constitutional level.[7]

---

[6] Serras v. First Tennessee Bank Nat. Ass'n 875 F.2d 1212, 1214 (6th Cir). Also Chenault v Walker, et al. No. W1998-00769-SC-R11-CV, TN Supreme Court, "the exercise of jurisdiction must comport with the United States Constitution."

[7] In our Petition for Removal, we requested that the district court rule on whether or not the state court has personal jurisdiction over the Kinneys'. This request was unanswered at the time of the remand.

C. The District Court Proceedings

Respondent made two specific false representations to the District Court that we believe had a direct bearing on its decision to remand the case.

1. Respondent attested to the existence of an Anderson Lumber credit application fully executed by the Petitioners.

On October 18, 2017, during a hearing held at the District Court in Knoxville, TN, Petitioner William Kinney explained to the court that the Respondent did not possess any documentation for the account sued upon in state court. Judge Guyton then asked the Respondent's counsel, Kizer & Black, Attorneys, "Counsel, do you have a completed, filled-out, signed Anderson Lumber Company credit application from any of these parties?" Atty. Melanie E. Davis of Kizer & Black, Attorneys, told the court, "There's a copy of it somewhere around the office." Atty. Morton (also of Kizer & Black) responded: "To my knowledge, Your Honor, there was, but I don't have it here in front of me to actually confirm." [8] Both responses were

---

[8] Case No. 3:16-cv-00078, Transcript Page 33, lines 9-16.

judicial admissions meant to assert the truth of a matter to the district court. Neither Attorney produced the requested documentation at said hearing, so the court issued an order for the Respondent to produce "the Anderson lumber credit application," and "any documents that support an existence of the account." [9] The respondent failed to comply with the order right up until January 9, 2018, when the case was remanded. Both Judicial admissions were meant to conceal the respondent's fraudulent claim, suborn Mr. Coleman's perjured Sworn Account, and to mislead the district court into believing that the respondent's state case was valid, and the state court had lawful jurisdiction over the petitioners.[10] Respondent's actions constitute Fraud Upon the Court, and its counsel hoodwinked the district court into remanding the case to state court. [11]

---

[9] Case No. 3:16-cv-00078, DOC 54, Page ID #: 1058.

[10] Petitioners also claimed in the removal petition that respondent violated the Fair Debt ollection Practices Act, 15 U.S. Code § 1692i(a)(2)(A), which requires a debt collector to bring an action in the judicial district upon which the consumer signed the contract sued upon. Respondent produced no such contract.

[11] Demjanjuk v. Petrovsky, 10 F.3d 338, 348 (6th Cir.

9

2. Respondent gave a false recitation of the chronological order of events leading up to removal, in Order to Mislead the District Court.

When asked about the status of the state case, the respondent stated that after the hearing held in state court to set the trial date, the case was then "immediately removed." However, the correct sequence of events begins with (1) the ex parte hearing held by the respondent in state court on June 12, 2017, (2) the removal to district court on July 7, 2017, and (3) the ex parte hearing held by the respondent in state court to set a trial date on August 7, 2017. At the hearing held by the District Court on October 18, 2017, Judge Guyton asked the respondent's counsel, [clarifying remarks in brackets] "What's the status in state court?" [12] Atty. Morton answered, "The status of the state court is, The Court dismissed Ms. Kinney's counterclaims,

---

1993). This standard recognizes that fraud upon the court, unlike perjury, need not be based on affirmative misstatements, but may be based on nondisclosures, and need not be based on proof of subjective knowledge of falsity, but may be founded on a showing of willful blindness or reckless disregard for the truth.

[12] Case No. 3:16-cv-00078, Transcript Page 12, lines 8-9

[this dismissal occurred at the hearing held on June 12, 2017[13]]

and at that point, while I was in the courtroom, the Judge said, "Let's go ahead and give notice and set this motion for trial." I did that, a hearing for setting the trial,

[the hearing for setting the trial date was held on August 7, 2017]

and immediately then the case was again removed here to the federal court."[14]

In fact, the removal had already occurred at the time of the August 7, 2017 hearing. Surprisingly, the remand order refers only to the hearing held on August 7, 2017, as shown below;

"Defendants also missed the window for removal under § 1446(b)(3), as the only filings in the underlying state case within thirty days of the filing of the petition for removal are a motion to set trial and a notice of hearing –

---

[13] Case No 3:17-cv-00288, DOC 1, Page ID #: 53

[14] Transcript Page 13, line 13-25, and Page 14, lines 1-2.

neither of which would cause a case not originally subject to removal to later become subject to removal. Defendants' petition for removal was thus untimely."

The basis for the removal is completely misapprehended by the district court when it refers to the August 7, 2017 hearing as the only filing that occurred during the statutory 30-day period for removal. Consequently, the remand order omits the Petitioner's stated reason for the removal, namely the June 12, 2017 *ex parte* hearing. Atty. Morton's recitation of the events, which also omits the June 12, 2017 hearing, appears to have been wrongly adopted by the district court. The Petitioners "Introduction" to the Complaint and Memorandum in Support of Removal, states that on June 12, 2017, the state court held an unlawful hearing scheduled by respondents, which supported removal to federal court. [15]

---

[15] Case No, 2:17-cv-00288, DOC 1, Page ID# 11

D. The Appellate Court Proceedings

The Sixth Circuit denied our appeal for "failure to file a timely notice of removal," pursuant to 28 U.S.C. § 1446(b)(1), which states, "notice must be filed within 30 days after the receipt by the defendant . . . of a copy of the initial pleading." This is the same reason and statutory provision stated by the district court in its remand order, which is also the same reason and statutory provision stated in the respondent's motion to remand. However, 28 U.S.C. § 1446(b)(1), is inapplicable to the circumstances that prompted the removal. Our Petition for Removal specifically invokes 28 U.S.C. § 1446(b)(3), on the basis that the *ex parte* hearing held on June 12, 2017, and subsequent court order, violated our federal constitutional rights. Our Petition for Removal under § 1441(a), vested federal jurisdiction based on the requirement of 28 U.S.C. § 1446(b)(3), and jurisdiction should not have been divested by the respondent's claim pertaining to an irrelevant process found in § 1446(b)(1).

In addition to this, and specifically citing to *Barlow*, we requested that the Sixth Circuit view our appeal in the same way it would view a Rule 60(b)(3) motion and vacate the remand order for discovery fraud, attorney misconduct, and Fraud Upon the Court.[16] In response, the Sixth Circuit stated in its order that the special circumstances allowing for the appeal of a remand order, were not applicable to our case. We believe the appeals court misapprehended the nature of our appeal, which was a request to vacate the remand for fraud. Our appeal did not reach the merits of the remand order, but rather, only the means in which the respondent obtained the remand. The reason for the denial of our appeal is inconsistent with the ruling made by the Fourth Circuit in the case of *Barlow*. The Fourth Circuit reasoned that a remand order can be vacated on the ground of attorney misconduct and fraud which led up to the remand. In the case of *Barlow*, the Plaintiff made false representations in court, to destroy diversity

---

[16] Rule 60(b) is not preserving an action confined by the elements of the crime of perjury. It is preserving a broader remedy for deceit directed at the court itself. This Court's leading decision on "fraud upon the court," Hazel-Atlas Glass Co. v. Hartford-Empire Co., 322 U.S. 238 (1944), makes this clear.

jurisdiction and keep her case in state court. In a similar manner, in the instant case, the respondent made false representations to the district court in order to obtain a remand and keep its case in state court.[17]

REASONS WHY CERTIORARI SHOULD BE GRANTED

I.

The District Court Exceeded Its Statutory Authority by Issuing the Remand Sua Sponte

As stated in Section D above, the respondent moved the district court to remand this case pursuant to 28 U.S. Code § 1446(b)(1), which was irrelevant to our claim for removal.[18]

---

[17] The removal and subsequent remand of this case included the seizure and disposition of petitioner's property by the state court without due process, in violation of the Fourth Amendment.

[18] Respondents Motion to Remand, Case 3:17-cv-00288, DOC4, Page ID #: 121

The district court referred to this same provision and further stated in its remand order that we also "missed the window for removal under § 1446(b)(3)," which is not a claim made by the respondent. Subsequently, the district court remanded our case sua sponte under § 1446(b)(3), and not for the reason given by the respondent under § 1446(b)(1). The Ninth Circuit recently ruled in Kenny v Wal-Mart Stores, Inc., "...a district court lacks authority to sua sponte remand an action unless there is a defect in subject matter jurisdiction."[19] Federal subject matter jurisdiction was not an issue in our appeal. This Court concluded in Thermtron that only remand orders issued under § 1447(c) and invoking the grounds specified therein . . . . . are immune from review under § 1447(d)."[20] The grounds specified under § 1447(c) and pertaining to "any defect other than lack of subject matter jurisdiction," are itemized in § 1446(b)(1) and (b)(3). The respondent's motion to

---

[19] Kenny v Wal-Mart Stores, Inc., et al., 2018 WL 650998 (9th Cir. Feb. 1, 2018)

[20] Thermtron Products, Inc. v. Hermansdorfer, 423 U.S. 336 Id. at 346.

remand did not invoke § 1446(b)(3) and should therefore be reviewable. The Sixth Circuit ruled in Page, that "such an error is subject to appellate review."[21]

II.

The Remand Order Created Appealable Collateral Issues Left Undecided By The Appeals Court

The district court based its remand entirely on the August 7, 2017 hearing in state court, and did not consider the state court hearing held on June 12, 2017, which has become a collateral issue involving substantive rights under the federal constitution.[22] The Fourth Circuit ruled in Barlow (regarding this same issue), that review of a "collateral decision that is [logically and factually] severable from the remand order" and that had a "conclusive effect upon the parties' substantive rights," is reviewable. Section 1447(d) does not prohibit vacating an order as prohibited by Rule 60(b)(3); it merely prohibits reviewing an order.[23]

---

[21] Page v. City of Southfield; 45 F.3d 128, 6TH Circuit ('remand(ing) a case sua sponte for a perceived defect in removal procedure… is subject to appellate review.')

²² On June 8, 2018, Petitioners filed another case in Federal Court to address the deprivation of our civil and equal rights that occurred at the hearing on June 12, 2017 at state court (Case No. 3:18-cv-00227), which was not addressed by the district court in its remand order of January 9, 2018.. The filing of this complaint was necessary in order to preserve our federal rights before our claim was barred by the Statute of Limitations, which runs for one year in the State of Tennessee.

²³ Barlow v. Colgate Palmolive Co. 772 F.3d 1001, at 1009 (4th Cir. 2014) (en banc)...the types of relief provided by Rule 11 and Rule 60(b)(3) do not involve "review" as proscribed by § 1447(d).

A vacatur of a remand would not be wholly inconsistent with this court's position that a district court has jurisdiction to impose sanctions that are "collateral to the merits." once it has remanded an action to state court.²⁴ It is therefore reasonable to conclude that Rule 60(b)(3) analysis is not precluded by § 1447(d).²⁵

---

²⁴ Cooter & Gell v. Hartmarx Corp., 496 U.S. 384, 389-90, also, Willy v. Coastal Corp.: 503 U.S. 131, 137]

²⁵ Schultz v Butcher, 24 F.3d 626 (1994)

In addition to this, the false representations made to the District Court by Atty.'s Davis and Morton were judicial admissions made about factual contentions and subject to Rule 11 sanctions as a collateral issue. Four days preceding the remand, the petitioners had moved the district court for sanctions for contempt, and sanctions pursuant to F.R.C.P., Rule 16(f) and Rule 11, for non-compliance with a court order which was unanswered at the time of the remand, and was not reviewed by the Sixth Circuit during appeal.

III.

Review Is Warranted Because

Fraud Vitiates Everything.

Gain that is accomplished by fraud goes against the legal principle that "no man should be allowed to take advantage of his own fraud," and courts do not reward misbehavior by those appearing before them. A wrongdoer should be deprived of his ill-gotten gain, and no one who comes to court with unclean hands should be permitted to make any claim upon his own inequity. Judicial estoppel protects the judicial process, and fraud upon the court is presumably the worst offense against that process. When the judicial process is corrupted by officers of the court, there has been no equitable adjudication made by the court, and the court must use its remedial power to undo the harm that if left undone, damages the integrity of the court itself. A remand order procured by fraud upon the court, is not one that is erroneous [26] or the result of legal error.[27] It is based on calculated misrepresentations of the facts of a case. Attorney misconduct effects the Judges ability to act impartially, in good faith, and in accordance with the law. For this reason, a remand order based upon a corrupted decisional process, should be subject to vacatur because it attacks the way in which the respondent secured the remand order, not the merits or correctness of the orders themselves."[28]

---

[26] Thermtron Prods., Inc., 423 U.S. at 343

[27] Kircher v. Putnam Funds Trust 547 U.S 633, at 634

[28] Barlow, 772 F.3d 1012

IV.

Review Is Warranted Because Only This Court Can Decide a Circuit Split.

In the current case, the attorneys deliberately misstated facts and attested to the existence of evidence that does not in fact exist, in order to defeat Petitioners removal. If those same attorneys can further rely on the removal statute's no-review directive to avoid accountability, not only have the Petitioners suffered the deprivation of federal rights, the integrity of the justice system has also been diminished. It is not unreasonable to suggest that if this case were under the jurisdiction of the Fourth Circuit, there is a strong possibility that the remand order at issue would have been vacated and our constitutional rights preserved in federal court. It is under these circumstances the Fourth Circuit reasoned that vacatur of a remand order that has been deceptively induced is not a "review" forbidden by Congress. When Congress enacted, <u>The Jurisdiction and Removal Act of 1875</u>, it intended removal to be a means to protect federal constitutional rights against state court prejudice and local influence, such as those encountered by the Petitioners. At the same time, Section 1447 (and its predecessor) was meant to safeguard the process by allowing a district court to distinguish between a properly removed case, and one that has been removed to delay and frustrate justice. However, the Petitioners say to this court, these two concerns should also be considered alongside a third possibility, namely that a properly removed case might be remanded due to fraud.

CONCLUSION

Based on the foregoing, Petitioners respectfully submit that this Petition for Writ of Certiorari should be granted. The Court may wish to consider summary reversal of the decision of the Sixth Circuit Court of Appeals.

Submitted this 10th day of September, 2018.

_____

William Kinney

_____

Margaret Kinney

CERTIFICATE OF COMPLIANCE

I certify that this brief is in compliance with the Rules of the Supreme Court of the United States, and contains 3,556 words, excluding the table of contents, table of authorities, constitutional provisions and statutes, rules or regulations, appendix, and certificate of service.

Certificate of Service:

A copy of this document has been sent to counsel for the respondent, via USPS Certified Mail;

McDonald, Levy, & Taylor; Attorneys at Law

10805 Kingston Pike Suite #200

Knoxville, TN 37934

CERTIFIED MAIL RECEIPT NO.

7016 1370 0000 3637 0736

Kizer & Black, Attorneys, PLLC

217 East Broadway Avenue

Maryville, TN 37804

CERTIFIED MAIL RECEIPT NO.

7016 1370 0000 3637 0743

24

APPENDIX

ORDERS

Order Denying Hearing En Banc

No. 18-5150 - Filed: 07/10/2018

UNITED STATES COURT OF APPEALS FOR THE SIXTH CIRCUIT

ANDERSON LUMBER COMPANY, INC., Plaintiff-Appellee, v.

WILLIAM KINNEY; MARGARET KINNEY, Defendants-Appellants.

O R D E R

BEFORE: SILER, COOK, and WHITE, Circuit Judges.

The court received a petition for rehearing en banc. The original panel has reviewed the petition for rehearing and concludes that the issues raised in the petition were fully considered upon the original submission and decision of the case. The petition then was circulated to the full court. No judge has requested a vote on the suggestion for rehearing en banc. Therefore, the petition is denied.

ENTERED BY ORDER OF THE COURT Deborah

S. Hunt, Clerk

Case: 18-5150 Document: 15-1 Filed: 07/10/2018 Page: 1

Order Denying Appeal

No. 18-5150 - Filed: 03/28/2018

UNITED STATES COURT OF APPEALS FOR THE SIXTH CIRCUIT

ANDERSON LUMBER COMPANY, INC., Plaintiff-Appellee, v.

WILLIAM KINNEY; MARGARET KINNEY, Defendants-Appellants.

O R D E R

Before: SILER, COOK, and WHITE, Circuit Judges.

This matter is before the court upon initial consideration to determine whether this appeal was taken from an appealable order. Anderson Lumber Company, Inc. commenced this action in Tennessee state court in November of 2012. In July of 2017, defendants William and Margaret Kinney ("the Kinneys") attempted to remove the case to federal court. By order entered on January 9, 2018, the district court remanded the case to state court for failure to file a timely notice of removal. See 28 U.S.C. § 1446(b) (notice must "be filed within 30 days after the receipt by the defendant . . . of a copy of the initial pleading"); Things Remembered, Inc. v. Petrarca, 516 U.S. 124, 128 (1995) ("untimely removal[] [is] precisely the type of removal defect contemplated by § 1447(c)"). The Kinneys now appeal the district court's remand. A district court order remanding a case to the state court from which it was removed is not appealable absent special circumstances, not applicable here. See 28 U.S.C. § 1447(d); Things Remembered, Inc., 516 U.S. at 128 We therefore DISMISS the appeal. ENTERED BY ORDER OF THE COURT Deborah S. Hunt, Clerk

Case: 18-5150 Document: 10-2 Filed: 03/28/2018 Page: 2

Order Remanding Case to State Court

UNITED STATES DISTRICT COURT EASTERN DISTRICT OF TENNESSEE

ANDERSON LUMBER COMPANY, INC., Plaintiff, v.

WILLIAM KINNEY and MARGARET KINNEY, Defendants.

No.:3:17-CV-288-TAV-HBG

ORDER

Before the Court are plaintiff's motions to remand [Docs. 4, 5], to which defendants responded [Doc. 6]. For the reasons explained below, the Court will grant plaintiff's motion to remand, and remand this case to the Circuit Court for Blount County, Tennessee.

Pursuant to 28 U.S.C. § 1446(b)(1), a defendant may file a notice of removal within thirty days of receiving the initial pleading, or within thirty days of receiving a summons if the initial pleading need not be served on the defendant, whichever period is shorter. Additionally, pursuant to § 1446(b)(3), a defendant may file a notice of removal within thirty days of the defendant receiving notice that a case which was not originally subject to removal has become subject to removal, via "an amended pleading, motion, order, or other paper from which it may first be ascertained that the case is one which is or has become removable."

The underlying state-court action was filed on November 21, 2012 [Doc. 1 p. 71], and defendants were served in December 2012. The petition for removal was filed on July 7, 2017 [Doc. 1]. Defendants thus missed the window for removal under § 1446(b)(1). Defendants also missed the window for removal under § 1446(b)(3), as the only filings in the underlying state case within thirty days of the filing of the petition for removal are a motion to set trial and a notice of hearing, neither of which would cause a case not originally subject to removal to later become subject to removal. Defendants' petition for removal was thus untimely. Although defendants argue they suffered violations of their civil rights and the Fair Debt Collection Practices Act in June 2012 [Doc. 6], these alleged violations do not support removal under § 1446(b)(3), as they are not "an amended pleading, motion, order, or other paper from which it may first be ascertained that the case is one which is or has become removable." For these reasons, the Court GRANTS plaintiff's motions to remand this action

[Docs. 4, 5] and REMANDS this action to the Circuit Court for Blount County, Tennessee. The Court DENIES plaintiff's request for attorney's fees, finding such relief unwarranted at this time. The Court cautions defendants, however, that any further erroneous attempts to remove this case to federal court will result in an order of attorney's fees to plaintiff, as defendants have previously attempted to remove this case once before [See Case No. 3:15cv-324 (attempting to remove Blount County Circuit Court Case No. E-24747)]. The Clerk of Court is DIRECTED to CLOSE this case.

IT IS SO ORDERED.

s/ Thomas A. Varlan

CHIEF UNITED STATES DISTRICT JUDGE

CONSTITUTIONAL PROVISIONS

First Amendment To The United States Constitution,

"Congress shall make no law respecting an establishment of religion, or prohibiting the free exercise thereof; or abridging the freedom of speech, or of the press; or the right of people peaceably to assemble, and to petition the government for a redress of grievances."

Fourth Amendment To The United States Constitution.

"The right of the people to be secure in their persons, houses, papers, and effects, against unreasonable searches and seizures, shall not be violated, and no Warrants shall issue, but upon probable cause, supported by Oath or affirmation, and particularly describing the place to be searched, and the persons or things to be seized."

Fourteenth Amendment To The United States Constitution, Section I,

"No state shall make or enforce any law which shall abridge the privileges or immunities of citizens of the United States; nor shall any state deprive any person of life, liberty, or property, without due process of law; nor deny to any person within its jurisdiction the equal protection of the laws."

STATUTES

28 U.S. Code § 1254 - Courts of appeals; certiorari; certified questions

Cases in the courts of appeals may be reviewed by the Supreme Court by the following methods:

(1) By writ of certiorari granted upon the petition of any party to any civil or criminal case, before or after rendition of judgment or decree;

28 U.S. Code § 1446 - Procedure for removal of civil actions (a)Generally.—A defendant or defendants desiring to remove any civil action from a State court shall file in the district court of the United States for the district and division within which such action is pending a notice of removal signed pursuant to Rule

11 of the Federal Rules of Civil Procedure and containing a short and plain statement of the grounds for removal, together with a copy of all process, pleadings, and orders served upon such defendant or defendants in such action. (b)Requirements; Generally.—(1) The notice of removal of a civil action or proceeding shall be filed within 30 days after the receipt by the defendant, through service or otherwise, of a copy of the initial pleading setting forth the claim for relief upon which such action or proceeding is based, or within 30 days after the service of summons upon the defendant if such initial pleading has then been filed in court and is not required to be served on the defendant, whichever period is shorter. (2)(A) When a civil action is removed solely under section 1441(a), all defendants who have been properly joined and served must join in or consent to the removal of the action. (B) Each defendant shall have 30 days after receipt by or service on that defendant of the initial pleading or summons described in paragraph (1) to file the notice of removal. (C) If defendants are served at different times, and a later-served defendant files a notice of removal, any earlier-served defendant may consent to the removal even though that earlier-served defendant did not previously initiate or consent to removal. (3) Except as provided in subsection (c), if

the case stated by the initial pleading is not removable, a notice of removal may be filed within thirty days after receipt by the defendant, through service or otherwise, of a copy of an amended pleading, motion, order or other paper from which it may first be ascertained that the case is one which is or has become removable. (c) Requirements; Removal Based on Diversity of Citizenship.—(1) A case may not be removed under subsection (b)(3) on the basis of jurisdiction conferred by section 1332 more than 1 year after commencement of the action, unless the district court finds that the plaintiff has acted in bad faith in order to prevent a defendant from removing the action. (2) If removal of a civil action is sought on the basis of the jurisdiction conferred by section 1332(a), the sum demanded in good faith in the initial pleading shall be deemed to be the amount in controversy, except that— (A) the notice of removal may assert the amount in controversy if the initial pleading seeks— (i) nonmonetary relief; or (ii) a money judgment, but the State practice either does not permit demand for a specific sum or permits recovery of damages in excess of the amount demanded; and (B) removal of the action is proper on the basis of an amount in controversy asserted under subparagraph (A) if the district court finds, by the preponderance of the evidence, that the amount in controversy exceeds the amount specified in section 1332(a). (3) (A) If the case stated by the initial pleading is not removable solely because the amount in controversy does not exceed the amount specified in section 1332(a), information relating to the amount in controversy in the record of the State proceeding, or in responses to discovery, shall be treated as an "other paper" under subsection (b)(3). (B) If the notice of removal is filed more than 1 year after commencement of the action and the district court finds that the plaintiff deliberately failed to disclose the actual amount in controversy to prevent removal, that finding shall be deemed bad faith under paragraph (1). (d)Notice to Adverse Parties and State Court.—Promptly after the filing of such notice of removal of a civil action the defendant or defendants shall give written notice thereof to all adverse parties and shall file a copy of the notice with the clerk of such State court, which shall effect the removal and the State court shall proceed no further unless and until the case is remanded. (e)Counterclaim in 337 Proceeding.—With respect to any counterclaim removed to a district court pursuant to section 337(c) of the Tariff Act of 1930, the district court shall resolve such counterclaim in the same manner as an original complaint under the Federal Rules of Civil Procedure, except that the payment of a filing fee shall not be required in such cases and the counterclaim shall relate back to the date of the original complaint in the proceeding before the International Trade Commission under section 337 of that Act. (g) [1] Where the civil action or criminal prosecution that is removable under section 1442(a) is a proceeding in which a judicial order for testimony or documents is sought or issued or sought to be enforced, the 30-day requirement of subsection (b) of this section and paragraph (1) of section 1455(b) is satisfied if the person or entity desiring to remove the proceeding files the notice of removal not later than 30 days after receiving, through service, notice of any such proceeding.

28 U.S. Code § 1447 - Procedure after removal generally (a) In any case removed from a State court, the district court may issue all necessary orders and process to bring before it all proper parties whether served by process issued by the State court or otherwise. (b) It may require the removing party to file with its clerk copies of all records and proceedings in such State court or may cause the same to be brought before it by writ of certiorari issued to such State court. (c) A motion to remand the case on the basis of any defect other than lack of subject matter jurisdiction must be made within 30 days after the filing of the notice of removal under section 1446(a). If at any time before final judgment it appears that the district court lacks subject matter jurisdiction, the case shall be remanded. An order remanding the case may require payment of just costs and any actual expenses, including attorney fees, incurred as a result of the removal. A certified copy of the order of remand shall be mailed by the clerk to the clerk of the State court. The State court may thereupon proceed with such case. (d) An order remanding a case to the State court from which it was removed is not reviewable on appeal or otherwise, except that an order remanding a case to the State court from which it was removed pursuant to section 1442 or 1443 of this title shall be reviewable by appeal or otherwise. (e) If after removal the plaintiff seeks to join additional defendants whose joinder would destroy subject matter jurisdiction, the court may deny joinder, or permit joinder and remand the action to the State court.

42 U.S. Code § 1983 - Civil action for deprivation of rights Every person who, under color of any statute, ordinance, regulation, custom, or usage, of any State or Territory or the District of Columbia, subjects, or causes to be subjected, any citizen of the United States or other person within the jurisdiction thereof to the deprivation of any rights, privileges, or immunities secured by the

Constitution and laws, shall be liable to the party injured in an action at law, suit in equity, or other proper proceeding for redress, except that in any action brought against a judicial officer for an act or omission taken in such officer's judicial capacity, injunctive relief shall not be granted unless a declaratory decree was violated or declaratory relief was unavailable.

15 U.S. Code § 1692i(a)(2)(A). (a) Venue;

Any debt collector who brings any legal action on a debt against any consumer shall—(1) in the case of an action to enforce an interest in real property securing the consumer's obligation, bring such action only in a judicial district or similar legal entity in which such real property is located; or (2) in the case of an action not described in paragraph (1), bring such action only in the judicial district or similar legal entity—(A) in which such consumer signed the contract sued upon; or (B) in which such consumer resides at the commencement of the action. (b) Authorization of actions Nothing in this subchapter shall be construed to authorize the bringing of legal actions by debt collectors.

www.ingramcontent.com/pod-product-compliance
Lightning Source LLC
Chambersburg PA
CBHW070943220526
45469CB00007B/2495